YOUR KNOWLEDGE HAS VALUE

AF151360

Irina Giertz

T.S. Eliot and the Peak of Modernism

GRIN Publishing

Bibliographic information published by the German National Library:

The German National Library lists this publication in the National Bibliography; detailed bibliographic data are available on the Internet at http://dnb.dnb.de .

Imprint:

Copyright © 2005 GRIN Verlag GmbH
Print and binding: Books on Demand GmbH, Norderstedt Germany
ISBN: 978-3-656-85133-2

GRIN - Your knowledge has value

Since its foundation in 1998, GRIN has specialized in publishing academic texts by students, college teachers and other academics as e-book and printed book. The website www.grin.com is an ideal platform for presenting term papers, final papers, scientific essays, dissertations and specialist books.

Visit us on the internet:

http://www.grin.com/

http://www.facebook.com/grincom

http://www.twitter.com/grin_com

T.S. Eliot and the Peak of Modernism

T.S. Eliot (1888-1965)

"Rhapsody on a Windy Night" (1910)

"Portrait of a Lady" (1910)

"The Love Song of Alfred J. Prufrock" (1910-1911)

"Preludes" (1910-1911)

"Gerontion" (1919)

"The Waste Land" (1922)

"Ash Wednesday" (1930)

"The Four Quartets" (1936-1943)

References:

Iser, Wolfgang. "Image and Montage". In: *Immanente Ästhetik*. Iser, Wolfgang (ed.). 1966.

The Cambridge Companion to Modernism. 1999. Levenson, Michael (ed.).

1. Modernism

    1.1. Definition and comparison to other literary periods

    1.2. Characteristic perception and representation of reality

2. <u>Progressive traits in Eliot's poetry vs. tradition</u>

    2.1. New tasks of the modern poetry

    2.2. New themes

    2.3. New forms and techniques

    2.4. Tradition – religious and literary

3. <u>Eliot's poetry and contemporary film (themes, motifs, techniques)</u>

    3.1. French Impressionism

    3.2. German Expressionism

    3.3. Neo-Realism

    3.4. Soviet Montage

    3.5. Montage in T.S. Eliot's work

1. Modernism

evoked through historical and cultural factors: industrialisation, democratisation, urbanisation, war, technological change, development of natural science, psychology and psychoanalysis; emancipation of women; Marx, Freud and Darwin respectively changed established notions of the social, the individual and the natural.

Romance – in modern literature, i.e., from the latter part of the 18th through the 19th centuries, a romance is a work of prose fiction in which the scenes and incidents are more or less removed from common life and are surrounded by a halo of mystery, an atmosphere of strangeness and adventure.

Realism – literature that attempts to depict life in an entirely objective manner, without idealisation or glamour, and without didactic or moral ends. Realism may be said to have begun with such early English novelists as Defoe, Fielding, and Smollett, and to have become a definite literary trend in the 19th century.

Modernism is the art of the tradition of the new. It is experimental, formally complex, elliptical, and tends to associate notions of the artist's freedom from realism, materialism, traditional genre and form, with notions of cultural apocalypse and disaster. It is disputable when it starts (French symbolism; decadence; the break-up of naturalism) and whether it has ended. It can be regarded as a time-bound concept (from 1890 to 1930) or a timeless one (including Lawrence Sterne, John Donne, William Blake, Samuel Taylor Coleridge). The best focus remains a body of major writers: James, Conrad, Proust, Mann, Gide, Kafka, Svevo, Joyce, Musil, Faulkner in fiction; Strindberg, Pirandello, Wedekind, Brecht in drama; Mallarmé, Yeats, Eliot, Pound, Rilke, Stevens in poetry. Their works are aesthetically radical, contain striking technical innovations, emphasise spatial and rhythmic as opposed to chronological relations, tend towards ironic modes.

Postmodernism – the new avantgarde literature which partly carried modernism further, partly reacted against it – e.g., against its ideology and its historical orientation. What it consistently pretended to be and sometimes actually was was new. It was determinedly self-destructive and attempted to cut off its branch of the past, by proposing entirely new methods, a fresh canon of authors (Nietzsche, Freud, Saussure, Proust) and a new register of allusions.

Realism, according to many critics, is characterised by its attempt objectively to offer up **a mirror to the world**, thus disavowing its own culturally conditioned processes and ideological stylistic assumptions. It also, modelled on prose forms such as history and journalism, generally features characters, language and a spatial and temporal setting very familiar to its contemporary readers and often presents itself as transparently representative of the author's society. The hegemony of realism was challenged by Modernism and then postmodernism, as **alternative ways of representing reality** and the world. Realism itself was once a new, innovative form of writing, with authors such as Daniel Defoe (1660-1731) and Samuel Richardson (1690-1761) providing a different template for fiction from the previously dominant mode of prose writing, the Romance, which was parodied in one of the very first novels, Cervantes's *Don Quixote* (1605-1615).

Very broadly speaking, the vast majority of attempts to offer alternative modes of representation from the middle of the 19th century to the middle of the 20th century have at one time or another been termed Modernist, and this applies to literature, music, painting, film and architecture. In **poetry**, Modernism is associated with moves to break from the iambic pentameter as the basic unit of verse, to introduce *verse libre*, symbolism and other new forms of writing. In **prose**, Modernism is associated with attempts to render human subjectivity in ways more real than realism: to represent consciousness, perception, emotion, meaning and the individual's relation to society through interior monologue, stream of consciousness, tunnelling, defamiliarisation, rhythm, irresolution and other terms. Modern writers struggled to modify if not overturn existing modes of representation, partly by pushing them towards the abstract or the retrospective, and to express the new sensibilities of their time: in a compressed, condensed, complex literature of the city, of industry and technology, war, machinery and speed, mass markets and communication, of internationalism, the New Woman, the aesthete, the nihilist and the flâneur.

Change of the **perception of reality** and the function of art. The previous dominant modes were a poetics of mimesis, verisimilitude and realism. By contrast, Modernism marked a clear movement towards increased sophistication, studied mannerism, profound introversion, self-scepticism and general anti-representationalism. In art, Modernists progressively undermined realism in movements like Post-Impressionism, Expressionism, Cubism, Symbolism, Imagism, Dadaism, Futurism and Surrealism. Each presented a different way of viewing reality. In fiction new writers rejected several of the fundamentals of classic realism: a dependable narrator; the depiction of a fixed stable self; history as a progressive linear process; bourgeois politics, which advocated reform not radical change; the tying up of all narrative strands, or 'closure'. The Modernist inclination towards **the subjective and the individual** resulted from the recognised failure to provide comprehensive solutions for contemporary conflicts. This, in its turn, involved the shift from the portrayal of external events towards the subjective perception of individuals. The recipient gets the insight into the emotional and mental world of the character at a certain crucial moment of the character's life.

2. Progressive traits in Eliot's poetry

2.1. New Tasks of the Modern Poetry

Poetry regarded as craft with a poem as the object to work upon and to improve

Modern poetry should be the expression of the modern attitude – the observer is emphasised who perceives the world from different angles, the prevailing attitude is negative due to increasing isolation of people and loss of personal individuality

Attempt to express emotion directly

Objective correlative – "the only way of expressing emotion in the form of art is by finding an objective correlative – a set of objects, a situation, a chain if events which shall be the formula of that particular emotion"; in the objective correlative the experience loses its individual character and acquires universal application; a symbol explaining itself

The Waste Land gave expression to the modernism wave in England, which supported other arts, especially painting which had been caustically criticised before

2.2. New themes

Industrialisation

City (Barthes – a discourse on itself, semiotic of the city), prototype picture of the city through certain signs: sights, famous buildings and streets, sounds (motors, voices), weather (fog), crowd – already one of these signs helps the reader create the illusion of the city

Sexuality – unattainable purity, lust prevails, lack of feeling and love; love is highly idealised by Eliot (higher love otherwise coupling)

The role of women in the society – discrepancy between Mother and Woman, emancipation

Failure of communication due to the WW1, development of the mass society and loss of individuality; passivity of people, stagnation, fear of misunderstanding

Fears

Subjectivity of perception

2.3. New forms and techniques

Estrangement techniques – arts should not be easy to conceive, arts should activate and challenge the recipient to make out the meaning on one's own

Inner monologue (from the classic dramatic monologue: Browning)

Use of symbols and metaphors

Fragmented depiction of events as opposed to chronological, **montage/collage** as form - reflects the content: communication failure, disconnectedness of people and longing for love, warmth and understanding; the pictures evoked are only scarcely illuminated/ elucidated (cut, dissolve, fade), no explanations/exposition, the host of allusions confuse/irritate the reader – activity of the reader, density of the texture, extreme depth of some passages

Polyphony – a number of different voices (angles, points of view) belonging not necessarily to one and the same speaker, the identity of the lyrical I is problematic

Lack of exposition – the reader is expected to actively participate

verse libré – blank verse, iambic pentameter without rhyme

Expansive references to other writers and their works

2.4. Tradition – religious and literary

Crisis of values, superficiality, vulgarity, selfishness, hypocrisy, sexual promiscuity

Degradation, degeneration

Lack of spirituality and loss of faith, nihilism – solution: return to religion and faith, conscious suffering of losses to achieve salvation (problematic solution, criticised)

References to earlier authors and works in order to revive them and the values they advocated. Such allusions allow to convey the spirit of these works in an abridged form (a line of the poem). Eliot's allusions are taken from: Dante, die Bible, ancient Greek authors, Shakespeare, Middleton, Marvell; "The Waste Land" - Frazer *The Golden Bough*, Weston *From Ritual to Romance*; "The Four Quartets" - Augustin, Bernard von Clairvaux. The point was not the tradition established by these authors but the lost values which they stand for.

Case Study: "The Love Song of Alfred J. Prufrock" (1910-1911)

Portrait of the contemporary man, his problems and fears. Although living in a city, he appears lonesome and isolated. He longs for communication and love, and realises that he has to change his life to achieve it. He keeps on trying but always falls back into his accustomed ways. His conflict is provoked by the disparity between his wish for a fulfilled life and his fear of unpredictable reaction on part of other people should he really dare to reveal his own nature.

Influences: by French Symbolists and English metaphysic poets of the 17th century Donne and Marvell.

Parts:

The Evening - The Overwhelming Question – Michelangelo - The Fog - The Time - The Voices, the Eyes and the Arms - A Pair of Ragged Claws - John the Baptist - And would it have been worth it, after all – Hamlet - The Mermaids

General points of critic (traditional reader):

formlessness, lack of unity

utter pessimism

unintelligibility, obscurity

elitist writing

Points of appreciation (modern reader):

intelligent

realistic, honest

modern

an interesting rhyme scheme/metre

Common problem – Eliot's poems are difficult to understand

3. Eliot's poetry and contemporary film (themes, motifs, techniques)

3.1. French Impressionism (1918-1929)

Impressionists regarded art a a form to express individual impressions. Art cannot and should not present the truth, instead it expresses human experience which, in its turn, provokes feelings of the recipient. This stands in relation to Eliot's own technique of the objective correlative which stipulates that feelings and not experience should be directly expressed: Feeling overwhelms the text. Impressionism artworks evoke through depiction of landscapes transient emotions, impressions. The basis of many impressionism film is rather '*visual rhythm*' than plot.

Certain expressive means were applied to convey the subjectivity of the characters, which includes visions, dreams, or reminiscences. This was achieved through optic superimposition: filters, masks, concave or convex mirrors, unfocused shots etc. were used to convey subjectivity.

El Dorado, Marcel L'Herbier 1921 (dancer Sibilla)

3.2. German Expressionism (1920-1927)

Expressionism established in Europe as early as 1908 in painting and theatre, mostly in

Germany, as reaction against realism. It is characterised by extreme distortions of frames to show the inner emotions not the 'real' outward appearance. In film the expressionism emphasised the construction of the frame (mise-en-scene) and saw the frame as a graphic work of art – frames were extremely elaborated graphically. Decorations were mostly exotic or fantastic, to this end supernatural or mythological plots were taken, or lunatics as characters.

Das Cabinet des Dr. Caligari, Robert Wiene, 1920

3.3. Neo-realism (1927-1933)

Reaction against emotionality and supernatural themes of Expressionism.

One of the trends was the street film, in which characters from the middle class encounter in the street such social evils as prostitution, gambling, black market, etc. These films were very pessimistic due to their gloomy and desolate pictures.

Dirnentragödie, Bruno Rahn 1927

Metropolis, Fritz Lang 1926 – themes: city, industrialisation, power, sexuality; motifs of spirituality and decline

3.4. Soviet Montage (1917-1933)

Continuity editing established around 1910 in Hollywood; to achieve clarity and development of the plot; the main feature is the succession of frames: establishing shot – shot/reverse-shot to provide a seamless connection of frames.

Eisenstein developed another form of montage where the frames are cut from disparate stories so that the conflict between them is intended, in line with Marxist dialectic, where a major principle proclaims that the opposites collide and thus produce a higher synthesis. Such kind of montage was supposed to induce the viewer to see the conflict between the elements and to create a new concept. The meaning was to be constructed by means of metaphors which emerge from the collision of two disparate frames. In his collision montage Eisenstein saw the opportunity to construct films as cognitive processes

(Eisenstein wanted to film *Das Kapital* by Marx). **<u>Abstract ideas in *Four Quartets*!</u>**

To achieve more dynamics the takes were cut very short, certain actions and even movements were cut several times. Spatial, temporal and graphic discontinuity forced the recipient to actively participate in making out the meaning.

Der Streik. Sergej Eisenstein 1925

A widely known example of such montage is a film sequence from Eisenstein's *Stachka* ('The Strike', 1925) where the parallel cutting takes place from two different plots; in one a police officer violently strikes with his fists against the table and orders to shoot the workers, in the other a butcher strikes the bull with a knife to kill it. The first story refers directly to the plot of the film, the second metaphorically. The result of the parallel cutting is to present the massacre on the workers as a slaughter.

3.5. Montage in T.S. Eliot's work

Eliot's montage is predominantly based on **quotations** from the Western cultural heritage. Eliot describes this approach in his essay "Tradition and the Individual Talent". The revival of the literature of the past appears to him the only possibility for a modern poet. Quotations are removed from their original context and transplanted in the new surroundings which is either another quotation itself, or a trivial situation of the contemporary everyday life. The montage effect is produced from the alternation of quotations and trivial situations.

This is very similar to the film montage, especially that by Eisenstein.

In *The Waste Land* pieces of different narrative lines are assembled which brings about collision of disparate frames.

Another significant feature of the film montage is **the creation of the new reality**. This reality is produced by the cut which assembles pieces of frames in a new way thus creating a new representation of reality. The same happens in Eliot's poetry: the given reality – the literal text and the trivial situation – are cut into pieces which are put together according to certain compositional principles. This process changes the original meaning of the quotation as well as the function of the trivial situation.

Waste Land 1-18 "April... in the winter."

The pictures unfolding in this scene are distinct and at the same time vague. A reflection over the threatening irrevocability of the change of seasons is followed by the exact name of the location, with weather details, which delineate the trite situation in the Hofgarten. Different persons are sketched and then take on definite shape, like in a close-up, due to the change from description to direct speech which is also done first in German and then in English. The close-up is dissolved immediately through the reminiscence of some action which took place somewhere else in the past. There is another close-up when this memory conveys a piece of the dialogue.

The arrangement of pictures in the sequence is determined through the cut, so that separate frames abruptly bump into each other. The pictures offered are rich in telling details but the cut prevents them from unfolding.